THE METAPHYSICAL ELEMENTS OF ETHICS

By

Immanuel Kant

.

INTRODUCTION TO THE METAPHYSICAL ELEMENTS OF ETHICS

Ethics in ancient times signified moral philosophy (philosophia moralis) generally, which was also called the doctrine of duties. Subsequently it was found advisable to confine this name to a part of moral philosophy, namely, to the doctrine of duties which are not subject to external laws (for which in German the name Tugendlehre was found suitable). Thus the system of general deontology is divided into that of jurisprudence (jurisprudentia), which is capable of external laws, and of ethics, which is not thus capable, and we may let this division stand.

I. Exposition of the Conception of Ethics

The notion of duty is in itself already the notion of a constraint of the free elective will by the law; whether this constraint be an external one or be self-constraint. The moral imperative, by its categorical (the unconditional ought) announces this constraint, which therefore does not apply to all rational beings (for there may also be holy beings), but applies to men as rational physical beings who are unholy enough to be seduced by pleasure to the transgression of the moral law, although they themselves recognize its authority; and when they do obey it, to obey it unwillingly (with resistance of their inclination); and it is in this that the constraint properly consists. Now, as man is a free (moral) being, the notion of duty can contain only self-constraint (by the idea of the law itself), when we look to the internal determination of the will (the spring), for thus only is it possible to combine that constraint (even if it were external) with the freedom of the elective will. The notion of duty then must be an ethical one.

The impulses of nature, then, contain hindrances to the fulfilment of duty in the mind of man, and resisting forces, some of them powerful; and he must judge himself able to combat these and to conquer them by means of reason, not in the future, but in the present, simultaneously with the thought; he must judge that he can do what the law unconditionally commands that he ought.

Now the power and resolved purpose to resist a strong but unjust opponent is called fortitude (fortitudo), and when concerned with the opponent of the moral character within us, it is virtue (virtus, fortitudo moralis). Accordingly, general deontology, in that part which brings not external, but internal, freedom under laws is the doctrine of virtue.

Jurisprudence had to do only with the formal condition of external freedom (the condition of consistency with itself, if its maxim became a universal law), that is, with law. Ethics, on the contrary, supplies us with a matter (an object of the free elective will), an end of pure reason which is at the same time conceived as an objectively necessary end, i.e., as duty for all men. For, as the sensible inclinations mislead us to ends (which are the matter of the elective will) that may contradict duty, the legislating reason cannot otherwise guard against their influence than by an opposite moral end, which therefore must be given a priori independently on inclination.

An end is an object of the elective will (of a rational being) by the idea of which this will is determined to an action for the production of this object. Now I may be forced by others to actions which are directed to an end as means, but I cannot be forced to have an end; I can only make something an end to myself. If, however, I am also bound to make something which lies in the notions of practical reason an end to myself, and therefore besides the formal determining principle of the elective will (as contained in law) to have also a material principle, an end which can be opposed to the end derived from sensible impulses; then this gives the notion of an end which is in itself a duty. The doctrine of this cannot belong to jurisprudence, but to ethics, since this alone includes in its conception self-constraint according to moral laws.

For this reason, ethics may also be defined as the system of the ends of the pure practical reason. The two parts of moral philosophy are distinguished as treating respectively of ends and of duties of constraint. That ethics contains duties to the observance of which one cannot be (physically) forced by others, is merely the consequence of this, that it is a doctrine of ends, since to be forced to have ends or to set them before one's self is a contradiction.

Now that ethics is a doctrine of virtue (doctrina officiorum virtutis) follows from the definition of virtue given above compared with the obligation, the peculiarity of which has just been shown. There is in fact no other determination of the elective will, except that to an end, which in the very notion of it implies that I cannot even physically be forced to it by the elective will of others. Another may indeed force me to do something which is not my end (but only means to the end of another), but he cannot force me to make it my own end, and yet I can have no end except of my own making. The latter supposition would be a contradiction- an act of freedom which yet at the same time would not be free. But there is no contradiction in setting before one's self an end which is also a duty: for in this case I constrain myself, and this is quite consistent with freedom. But how is such an end possible? That is now the question. For the possibility of the notion of the thing (viz., that it is not self-contradictory) is not enough to prove the possibility of the thing itself (the objective reality of the notion).

II. Exposition of the Notion of an End which is also a Duty

We can conceive the relation of end to duty in two ways; either starting from the end to find the maxim of the dutiful actions; or conversely, setting out from this to find the end which is also duty. Jurisprudence proceeds in the former way. It is left to everyone's free elective will what end he will choose for his action. But its maxim is determined a priori; namely, that the freedom of the agent must be consistent with the freedom of every other according to a universal law.

Ethics, however, proceeds in the opposite way. It cannot start from the ends which the man may propose to himself, and hence give directions as to the maxims he should adopt, that is, as to his duty; for that would be to take empirical principles of maxims, and these could not give any notion of duty; since this, the categorical ought, has its root in pure reason alone. Indeed, if the maxims were to be adopted in accordance with those ends (which are all selfish), we could not properly speak of the notion of duty at all. Hence in ethics the notion of duty must lead to ends, and must on moral principles give the foundation of maxims with respect to the ends which we ought to propose to ourselves.

Setting aside the question what sort of end that is which is in itself a duty, and how such an end is possible, it is here only necessary to show that a duty of this kind is called a duty of virtue, and why it is so called.

To every duty corresponds a right of action (facultas moralis generatim), but all duties do not imply a corresponding right (facultas juridica) of another to compel anyone, but only the duties called legal duties. Similarly to all ethical obligation corresponds the notion of virtue, but it does not follow that all ethical duties are duties of virtue. Those, in fact, are not so which do not concern so much a certain end (matter, object of the elective will), but merely that which is formal in the moral determination of the will (e.g., that the dutiful action must also be done from duty). It is only an end which is also duty that can be called a duty of virtue. Hence there are several of the latter kind (and thus there are distinct virtues); on the contrary, there is only one duty of the former kind, but it is one which is valid for all actions (only one virtuous disposition).

The duty of virtue is essentially distinguished from the duty of justice in this respect; that it is morally possible to be externally compelled to the latter, whereas the former rests on free self-constraint only. For finite holy beings (which cannot even be tempted to the violation of duty) there is no doctrine of virtue, but only moral philosophy, the latter being an autonomy of practical reason, whereas the former is also an autocracy of it. That is, it includes a consciousness- not indeed immediately perceived, but rightly concluded, from the moral categorical imperative- of the power to become master of one's inclinations which resist the law; so that human morality in its highest stage can yet be nothing more than virtue; even if it were quite pure (perfectly free from the influence of a spring foreign to duty), a state which is poetically personified under the name of the wise man (as an ideal to which one should continually approximate).

Virtue, however, is not to be defined and esteemed merely as habit, and (as it is expressed in the prize essay of Cochius) as a long custom acquired by practice of morally good actions. For, if this is not an effect of well-resolved and firm principles ever more and more purified, then, like any other mechanical arrangement brought about by technical practical reason, it is neither armed for all circumstances nor adequately secured against the change that may be wrought by new allurements.

REMARK

To virtue = + a is opposed as its logical contradictory (contradictorie oppositum) the negative lack of virtue (moral weakness) = 0; but vice = - a is its contrary (contrarie s. realiter oppositum); and it is not merely a needless question but an offensive one to ask whether great crimes do not perhaps demand more strength of mind than great virtues. For by strength of mind we understand the strength of purpose of a man, as a being endowed with freedom, and consequently so far as he is master of himself (in his senses) and therefore in a healthy condition of mind. But great crimes are paroxysms, the very sight of which makes the man of healthy mind shudder. The question would therefore be something like this: whether a man in a fit of madness can have more physical strength than if he is in his senses; and we may admit this without on that account ascribing to him more strength of mind, if by mind we understand the vital principle of man in the free use of his powers. For since those crimes have their ground merely in the power of the inclinations that weaken reason, which does not prove strength of mind, this question would be nearly the same as the question whether a man in a fit of illness can show more strength than in a healthy condition; and this may be directly denied, since the want of health, which consists in the proper balance of all the bodily forces of the man, is a weakness in the system of these forces, by which system alone we can estimate absolute health.

III. Of the Reason for conceiving an End which is also a Duty

An end is an object of the free elective will, the idea of which determines this will to an action by which the object is produced. Accordingly every action has its end, and as no one can have an end without himself making the object of his elective will his end, hence to have some end of actions is an act of the freedom of the agent, not an affect of physical nature. Now, since this act which determines an end is a practical principle which commands not the means (therefore not conditionally) but the end itself (therefore unconditionally), hence it is a categorical imperative of pure practical reason and one, therefore, which combines a concept of duty with that of an end in general.

Now there must be such an end and a categorical imperative corresponding to it. For since there are free actions, there must also be ends to which as an object those actions are directed. Amongst these ends there must also be some which are at the same time (that is, by their very notion) duties. For if there were none such, then since no actions can be without an end, all ends which practical reason might have would be valid only as means to other ends, and a categorical imperative would be impossible; a supposition which destroys all moral philosophy.

Here, therefore, we treat not of ends which man actually makes to himself in accordance with the sensible impulses of his nature, but of objects of the free elective will under its own laws- objects which he ought to make his end. We may call the former technical (subjective), properly pragmatical, including the rules of prudence in the choice of its ends; but the latter we must call the moral (objective) doctrine of ends. This distinction is, however, superfluous here, since moral philosophy already by its very notion is clearly separated from the doctrine of physical nature (in the present instance, anthropology). The latter resting on empirical principles, whereas the moral doctrine of ends which treats of duties rests on principles given a priori in pure practical reason.

IV. What are the Ends which are also Duties?

They are: A. OUR OWN PERFECTION, B. HAPPINESS OF OTHERS.

We cannot invert these and make on one side our own happiness, and on the other the perfection of others, ends which should be in themselves duties for the same person.

For one's own happiness is, no doubt, an end that all men have (by virtue of the impulse of their nature), but this end cannot without contradiction be regarded as a duty. What a man of himself inevitably wills does not come under the notion of duty, for this is a constraint to an end reluctantly adopted. It is, therefore, a contradiction to say that a man is in duty bound to advance his own happiness with all his power.

It is likewise a contradiction to make the perfection of another my end, and to regard myself as in duty bound to promote it. For it is just in this that the perfection of another man as a person consists, namely, that he is able of himself to set before him his own end according to his own notions of duty; and it is a contradiction to require (to make it a duty for me) that I should do something which no other but himself can do.

V. Explanation of these two Notions

A. OUR OWN PERFECTION

The word perfection is liable to many misconceptions. It is sometimes understood as a notion belonging to transcendental philosophy; viz., the notion of the totality of the manifold which taken together constitutes a thing; sometimes, again, it is understood as belonging to teleology, so that it signifies the correspondence of the properties of a thing to an end. Perfection in the former sense might be called quantitative (material), in the latter qualitative (formal) perfection. The former can be one only, for the whole of what belongs to the one thing is one. But of the latter there may be several in one thing; and it is of the latter property that we here treat.

When it is said of the perfection that belongs to man generally (properly speaking, to humanity), that it is in itself a duty to make this our end, it must be placed in that which may be the effect of one's deed, not in that which is merely an endowment for which we have to thank nature; for otherwise it would not be duty. Consequently, it can be nothing else than the cultivation of one's power (or natural capacity) and also of one's will (moral disposition) to satisfy the requirement of duty in general. The supreme element in the former (the power) is the understanding, it being the faculty of concepts, and, therefore, also of those concepts which refer to duty. First it is his duty to labour to raise himself out of the rudeness of his nature, out of his animal nature more and more to humanity, by which alone he is capable of setting before him ends to supply the defects of his ignorance by instruction, and to correct his errors;

he is not merely counselled to do this by reason as technically practical, with a view to his purposes of other kinds (as art), but reason, as morally practical, absolutely commands him to do it, and makes this end his duty, in order that he may be worthy of the humanity that dwells in him. Secondly, to carry the cultivation of his will up to the purest virtuous disposition, that, namely, in which the law is also the spring of his dutiful actions, and to obey it from duty, for this is internal morally practical perfection. This is called the moral sense (as it were a special sense, sensus moralis), because it is a feeling of the effect which the legislative will within himself exercises on the faculty of acting accordingly. This is, indeed, often misused fanatically, as though (like the genius of Socrates) it preceded reason, or even could dispense with judgement of reason; but still it is a moral perfection, making every special end, which is also a duty, one's own end.

B. HAPPINESS OF OTHERS

It is inevitable for human nature that man a should wish and seek for happiness, that is, satisfaction with his condition, with certainty of the continuance of this satisfaction. But for this very reason it is not an end that is also a duty. Some writers still make a distinction between moral and physical happiness (the former consisting in satisfaction with one's person and moral behaviour, that is, with what one does; the other in satisfaction with that which nature confers, consequently with what one enjoys as a foreign gift). Without at present censuring the misuse of the word (which even involves a contradiction), it must be observed that the feeling of the former belongs solely to the preceding head, namely, perfection. For he who is to feel himself happy in the mere consciousness of his uprightness already possesses that perfection which in the previous section was defined as that end which is also duty.

If happiness, then, is in question, which it is to be my duty to promote as my end, it must be the happiness of other men whose (permitted) end I hereby make also mine. It still remains left to themselves to decide what they shall reckon as belonging to their happiness; only that it is in my power to decline many things which they so reckon, but which I do not so regard, supposing that they have no right to demand it from me as their own. A plausible objection often advanced against the division of duties above adopted consists in setting over against that end a supposed obligation to study my own (physical) happiness, and thus making this, which is my natural and merely subjective end, my duty (and objective end). This requires to be cleared up.

Adversity, pain, and want are great temptations to transgression of one's duty; accordingly it would seem that strength, health, a competence, and welfare generally, which are opposed to that influence, may also be regarded as ends that are also duties; that is, that it is a duty to promote our own happiness not merely to make that of others our end. But in that case the end is not happiness but the morality of the agent; and happiness is only the means of removing the hindrances to morality; permitted means, since no one has a right to demand from me the sacrifice of my not immoral ends. It is not directly a duty to seek a competence for one's self; but indirectly it may be so; namely, in order to guard against poverty which is a great temptation to vice. But then it is not my happiness but my morality, to maintain which in its integrity is at once my end and my duty.

VI. Ethics does not supply Laws for Actions (which is done by

Jurisprudence), but only for the Maxims of Action

The notion of duty stands in immediate relation to a law (even though I abstract from every end which is the matter of the law); as is shown by the formal principle of duty in the categorical imperative: "Act so that the maxims of thy action might become a universal law." But in ethics this is conceived as the law of thy own will, not of will in general, which might be that of others; for in the latter case it would give rise to a judicial duty which does not belong to the domain of ethics. In ethics, maxims are regarded as those subjective laws which merely have the specific character of universal legislation, which is only a negative principle (not to contradict a law in general). How, then, can there be further a law for the maxims of actions?

It is the notion of an end which is also a duty, a notion peculiar to ethics, that alone is the foundation of a law for the maxims of actions; by making the subjective end (that which every one has)

subordinate to the objective end (that which every one ought to make his own). The imperative: "Thou shalt make this or that thy end (e. g., the happiness of others)" applies to the matter of the elective will (an object). Now since no free action is possible, without the agent having in view in it some end (as matter of his elective will), it follows that, if there is an end which is also a duty, the maxims of actions which are means to ends must contain only the condition of fitness for a possible universal legislation: on the other hand, the end which is also a duty can make it a law that we should have such a maxim, whilst for the maxim itself the possibility of agreeing with a universal legislation is sufficient.

For maxims of actions may be arbitrary, and are only limited by the condition of fitness for a universal legislation, which is the formal principle of actions. But a law abolishes the arbitrary character of actions, and is by this distinguished from recommendation (in which one only desires to know the best means to an end).

VII. Ethical Duties are of indeterminate, Juridical Duties of strict, Obligation

This proposition is a consequence of the foregoing; for if the law can only command the maxim of the actions, not the actions themselves, this is a sign that it leaves in the observance of it a latitude (latitudo) for the elective will; that is, it cannot definitely assign how and how much we should do by the action towards the end which is also duty. But by an indeterminate duty is not meant a permission to make exceptions from the maxim of the actions, but only the permission to limit one maxim of duty by another (e. g., the general love of our neighbour by the love of parents); and this in fact enlarges the field for the practice of virtue. The more indeterminate the duty, and the more imperfect accordingly the obligation of the man to the action, and the closer he nevertheless brings this maxim of obedience thereto (in his own mind) to the strict duty (of justice), so much the more perfect is his virtuous action.

Hence it is only imperfect duties that are duties of virtue. The fulfilment of them is merit (meritum) = + a; but their transgression is not necessarily demerit (demeritum) = - a, but only moral unworth = o, unless the agent made it a principle not to conform to those duties. The strength of purpose in the former case is alone properly called virtue [Tugend] (virtus); the weakness in the latter case is not vice (vitium), but rather only lack of virtue [Untugend], a want of moral strength (defectus moralis). (As the word Tugend is derived from taugen [to be good for something], Untugend by its etymology signifies good for nothing.) Every action contrary to duty is called transgression (peccatum). Deliberate transgression which has become a principle is what properly constitutes what is called vice (vitium).

Although the conformity of actions to justice (i.e., to be an upright man) is nothing meritorious, yet the conformity of the maxim of such actions regarded as duties, that is, reverence for justice is meritorious. For by this the man makes the right of humanity or of men his own end, and thereby enlarges his notion of duty beyond that of indebtedness (officium debiti), since although another man by virtue of his rights can demand that my actions shall conform to the law, he cannot demand that the law shall also contain the spring of these actions. The same thing is true of the general ethical command, "Act dutifully from a sense of duty." To fix this disposition firmly in one's mind and to quicken it is, as in the former case, meritorious, because it goes beyond the law of duty in actions and makes the law in itself the spring.

But just for or reason, those duties also must be reckoned as of indeterminate obligation, in respect of which there exists a subjective principle which ethically rewards them; or to bring them as near as possible to the notion of a strict obligation, a principle of susceptibility of this reward according to the law of virtue; namely, a moral pleasure which goes beyond mere satisfaction with oneself (which may be merely negative), and of which it is proudly said that in this consciousness virtue is its own reward.

When this merit is a merit of the man in respect of other men of promoting their natural ends, which are recognized as such by all men (making their happiness his own), we might call it the sweet merit, the consciousness of which creates a moral enjoyment in which men are by sympathy inclined to revel; whereas the bitter merit of promoting the true welfare of other men, even though they should not recognize it as such (in the case of the unthankful and ungrateful), has commonly no such reaction, but only produces a satisfaction with one's self, although in the latter case this would be even greater.

VIII. Exposition of the Duties of Virtue as Intermediate Duties

OUR OWN PERFECTION as an end which is also a duty

Physical perfection; that is, cultivation of all our faculties generally for the promotion of the ends set before us by reason. That this is a duty, and therefore an end in itself, and that the effort to effect this even without regard to the advantage that it secures us, is based, not on a conditional (pragmatic), but an unconditional (moral) imperative, may be seen from the following consideration. The power of proposing to ourselves an end is the characteristic of humanity (as distinguished from the brutes). With the end of humanity in our own person is therefore combined the rational will, and consequently the duty of deserving well of humanity by culture generally, by acquiring or advancing the power to carry out all sorts of possible ends, so far as this power is to be found in man; that is, it is a duty to cultivate the crude capacities of our nature, since it is by that cultivation that the animal is raised to man, therefore it is a duty in itself.

This duty, however, is merely ethical, that is, of indeterminate obligation. No principle of reason prescribes how far one must go in this effort (in enlarging or correcting his faculty of understanding, that is, in acquisition of knowledge or technical capacity); and besides the difference in the circumstances into which men may come makes the choice of the kind of employment for which he should cultivate his talent very arbitrary. Here, therefore, there is no law of reason for actions, but only for the maxim of actions, viz.: "Cultivate thy faculties of mind and body so as to be effective for all ends that may come in thy way, uncertain which of them may become thy own."

(b) Cultivation of Morality in ourselves. The greatest moral perfection of man is to do his duty, and that from duty (that the law be not only the rule but also the spring of his actions). Now at first sight this seems to be a strict obligation, and as if the principle of duty commanded not merely the legality of every action, but also the morality, i.e., the mental disposition, with the exactness and strictness of a law; but in fact the law commands even here only the maxim of the action, namely, that we should seek the ground of obligation, not in the sensible impulses (advantage or disadvantage), but wholly in the law; so that the action itself is not commanded. For it is not possible to man to see so far into the depth of his own heart that he could ever be thoroughly certain of the purity of his moral purpose and the sincerity of his mind even in one single action, although he has no doubt about the legality of it. Nay, often the weakness which deters a man from the risk of a crime is regarded by him as virtue (which gives the notion of strength). And how many there are who may have led a long blameless life, who are only fortunate in having escaped so many temptations. How much of the element of pure morality in their mental disposition may have belonged to each deed remains hidden even from themselves.

Accordingly, this duty to estimate the worth of one's actions not merely by their legality, but also by their morality (mental disposition), is only of indeterminate obligation; the law does not command this internal action in the human mind itself, but only the maxim of the action, namely, that we should strive with all our power that for all dutiful actions the thought of duty should be of itself an adequate spring.

HAPPINESS OF OTHERS as an end which is also a duty

Physical Welfare. Benevolent wishes may be unlimited, for they do not imply doing anything. But the case is more difficult with benevolent action, especially when this is to be done, not from friendly inclination (love) to others, but from duty, at the expense of the sacrifice and mortification of many of our appetites. That this beneficence is a duty results from this: that since our self-love cannot be separated from the need to be loved by others (to obtain help from them in case of necessity), we therefore make ourselves an end for others; and this maxim can never be obligatory except by having the specific character of a universal law, and consequently by means of a will that we should also make others our ends. Hence the happiness of others is an end that is also a duty.

I am only bound then to sacrifice to others a part of my welfare without hope of recompense: because it is my duty, and it is impossible to assign definite limits how far that may go. Much depends on what would be the true want of each according to his own feelings, and it must be left to each to determine this for himself. For that one should sacrifice his own happiness, his true wants, in order to promote that of others, would be a self-contradictory maxim if made a universal law. This duty, therefore, is only indeterminate; it has a certain latitude within which one may do more or less without our being able to assign its limits definitely. The law holds only for the maxims, not for definite actions.

Moral well-being of others (salus moralis) also belongs to the happiness of others, which it is our duty to promote, but only a negative duty. The pain that a man feels from remorse of conscience, although its origin is moral, is yet in its operation physical, like grief, fear, and every other diseased condition. To take care that he should not be deservedly smitten by this inward reproach is not indeed my duty but his business; nevertheless, it is my duty to do nothing which by the nature of man might seduce him to that for which his conscience may hereafter torment him, that is, it is my duty not to give him occasion of stumbling. But there are no definite limits within which this care for the moral satisfaction of others must be kept; therefore it involves only an indeterminate obligation.

IX. What is a Duty of Virtue?

Virtue is the strength of the man's maxim in his obedience to duty. All strength is known only by the obstacles that it can overcome; and in the case of virtue the obstacles are the natural inclinations which may come into conflict with the moral purpose; and as it is the man who himself puts these obstacles in the way of his maxims, hence virtue is not merely a self-constraint (for that might be an effort of one inclination to constrain another), but is also a constraint according to a principle of inward freedom, and therefore by the mere idea of duty, according to its formal law.

All duties involve a notion of necessitation by the law, and ethical duties involve a necessitation for which only an internal legislation is possible; juridical duties, on the other hand, one for which external legislation also is possible. Both, therefore, include the notion of constraint, either self-constraint or constraint by others. The moral power of the former is virtue, and the action springing from such a disposition (from reverence for the law) may be called a virtuous action (ethical), although the law expresses a juridical duty. For it is the doctrine of virtue that commands us to regard the rights of men as holy.

But it does not follow that everything the doing of which is virtue, is, properly speaking, a duty of virtue. The former may concern merely the form of the maxims; the latter applies to the matter of them, namely, to an end which is also conceived as duty. Now, as the ethical obligation to ends, of which there may be many, is only indeterminate, because it contains only a law for the maxim of actions, and the end is the matter (object) of elective will; hence there are many duties, differing according to the difference of lawful ends, which may be called duties of virtue (officia honestatis), just because they are subject only to free self-constraint, not to the constraint of other men, and determine the end which is also a duty.

Virtue, being a coincidence of the rational will, with every duty firmly settled in the character, is, like everything formal, only one and the same. But, as regards the end of actions, which is also duty, that is, as regards the matter which one ought to make an end, there may be several virtues; and as the obligation to its maxim is called a duty of virtue, it follows that there are also several duties of virtue.

The supreme principle of ethics (the doctrine of virtue) is: "Act on a maxim, the ends of which are such as it might be a universal law for everyone to have." On this principle a man is an end to himself as well as others, and it is not enough that he is not permitted to use either himself or others merely as means (which would imply that be might be indifferent to them), but it is in itself a duty of every man to make mankind in general his end.

The principle of ethics being a categorical imperative does not admit of proof, but it admits of a justification from principles of pure practical reason. Whatever in relation to mankind, to oneself, and others, can be an end, that is an end for pure practical reason: for this is a faculty of assigning ends in general; and to be indifferent to them, that is, to take no interest in them, is a contradiction; since in that case it would not determine the maxims of actions (which always involve an end), and consequently would cease to be practical reasons. Pure reason, however, cannot command any ends a priori, except so far as it declares the same to be also a duty, which duty is then called a duty of virtue.

X. The Supreme Principle of Jurisprudence was Analytical; that of Ethics is Synthetical

That external constraint, so far as it withstands that which hinders the external freedom that agrees with general laws (as an obstacle of the obstacle thereto), can be consistent with ends generally, is clear on the principle of contradiction, and I need not go beyond the notion of freedom in order to see it, let the end which each may be what he will. Accordingly, the supreme principle of jurisprudence is an analytical principle. On the contrary the principle of ethics goes beyond the notion of external freedom and, by general laws, connects further with it an end which it makes a duty. This principle, therefore, is synthetic. The possibility of it is contained in the Deduction (Sec. ix.).

This enlargement of the notion of duty beyond that of external freedom and of its limitation by the merely formal condition of its constant harmony; this, I say, in which, instead of constraint from without, there is set up freedom within, the power of self-constraint, and that not by the help of other inclinations, but by pure practical reason (which scorns all such help), consists in this fact, which raises it above juridical duty; that by it ends are proposed from which jurisprudence altogether abstracts. In the case of the moral imperative, and the supposition of freedom which it necessarily involves, the law, the power (to fulfil it) and the rational will that determines the maxim, constitute all the elements that form the notion of juridical duty. But in the imperative, which commands the duty of virtue, there is added, besides the notion of self-constraint, that of an end; not one that we have, but that we ought to have, which, therefore, pure practical reason has in itself, whose highest, unconditional end (which, however, continues to be duty) consists in this: that virtue is its own end and, by deserving well of men, is also its own reward. Herein it shines so brightly as an ideal to human perceptions, it seems to cast in the shade even holiness itself, which is never tempted to transgression. This, however, is an illusion arising from the fact that as we have no measure for the degree of strength, except the greatness of the obstacles which might have been overcome (which in our case are the inclinations), we are led to mistake the subjective conditions of estimation of a magnitude for the objective conditions of the magnitude itself. But when compared with human ends, all of which have their obstacles to be overcome, it is true that the worth of virtue itself, which is its own end, far outweighs the worth of all the utility and all the empirical ends and advantages which it may have as consequences.

> With all his failings, man is still
>
> Better than angels void of will.

We may, indeed, say that man is obliged to virtue (as a moral strength). For although the power (facultas) to overcome all imposing sensible impulses by virtue of his freedom can and must be presupposed, yet this power regarded as strength (robur) is something that must be acquired by the moral spring (the idea of the law) being elevated by contemplation of the dignity of the pure law of reason in us, and at the same time also by exercise.

XI. According to the preceding Principles, the Scheme of Duties of Virtue may be thus exhibited

The Material Element of the Duty of Virtue

Internal Duty of Virtue External Virtue of Duty

My Own End, The End of Others, which is also my the promotion of

Duty which is also my

Duty

(My own (The Happiness

Perfection) of Others)

The Law which is The End which is also Spring also Spring

On which the On which the

Morality Legality of every free determination of will rests

The Formal Element of the Duty of Virtue.

XII. Preliminary Notions of the Susceptibility of the Mind for Notions of Duty generally

These are such moral qualities as, when a man does not possess them, he is not bound to acquire them. They are: the moral feeling, conscience, love of one's neighbour, and respect for ourselves (self-esteem). There is no obligation to have these, since they are subjective conditions of susceptibility for the notion of duty, not objective conditions of morality. They are all sensitive and antecedent, but natural capacities of mind (praedispositio) to be affected by notions of duty; capacities which it cannot be regarded as a duty to have, but which every man has, and by virtue of which he can be brought under obligation. The consciousness of them is not of empirical origin, but can only follow on that of a moral law, as an effect of the same on the mind.

A. THE MORAL FEELING

This is the susceptibility for pleasure or displeasure, merely from the consciousness of the agreement or disagreement of our action with the law of duty. Now, every determination of the elective will proceeds from the idea of the possible action through the feeling of pleasure or displeasure in taking an interest in it or its effect to the deed; and here the sensitive state (the affection of the internal sense) is either a pathological or a moral feeling. The former is the feeling that precedes the idea of the law, the latter that which may follow it.

Now it cannot be a duty to have a moral feeling, or to acquire it; for all consciousness of obligation supposes this feeling in order that one may become conscious of the necessitation that lies in the notion of duty; but every man (as a moral being) has it originally in himself; the obligation, then, can only extend to the cultivation of it and the strengthening of it even by admiration of its inscrutable origin; and this is effected by showing how it is just, by the mere conception of reason, that it is excited most strongly, in its own purity and apart from every pathological stimulus; and it is improper to call this feeling a moral sense; for the word sense generally means a theoretical power of perception directed to an object; whereas the moral feeling (like pleasure and displeasure in general) is something merely subjective, which supplies no knowledge. No man is wholly destitute of moral feeling, for if he were totally unsusceptible of this sensation he would be morally dead; and, to speak in the language of physicians, if the moral vital force could no longer produce any effect on this feeling, then his humanity would be dissolved (as it were by chemical laws) into mere animality and be irrevocably confounded with the mass of other physical beings. But we have no special sense for (moral) good and evil any more than for truth, although such expressions are often used; but we have a susceptibility of the free elective will for being moved by pure practical reason and its law; and it is this that we call the moral feeling.

B. OF CONSCIENCE

Similarly, conscience is not a thing to be acquired, and it is not a duty to acquire it; but every man, as a moral being, has it originally within him. To be bound to have a conscience would be as much as to say to be under a duty to recognize duties. For conscience is practical reason which, in every case of law, holds before a man his duty for acquittal or condemnation; consequently it does not refer to an object, but only to the subject (affecting the moral feeling by its own act); so that it is an inevitable fact, not an obligation and duty. When, therefore, it is said, "This man has no conscience," what is meant is that he pays no heed to its dictates. For if he really had none, he would not take credit to himself for anything done according to duty, nor reproach himself with violation of duty, and therefore he would be unable even to conceive the duty of having a conscience.

I pass by the manifold subdivisions of conscience, and only observe what follows from what has just been said, namely, that there is no such thing as an erring conscience. No doubt it is possible sometimes to err in the objective judgement whether something is a duty or not; but I cannot err in the subjective whether I have compared it with my practical (here judicially acting) reason for the purpose of that judgement: for if I erred I would not have exercised practical judgement at all, and in that case there is neither truth nor error. Unconscientiousness is not want of conscience, but the propensity not to heed its judgement. But when a man is conscious of having acted according to his conscience, then, as far as regards guilt or innocence, nothing more can be required of him, only he is bound to enlighten his understanding as to what is duty or not; but when it comes or has come to action, then conscience speaks involuntarily and inevitably. To act conscientiously can, therefore, not be a duty, since otherwise it would be necessary to have a second conscience, in order to be conscious of the act of the first.

The duty here is only to cultivate our conscience, to quicken our attention to the voice of the internal judge, and to use all means to secure obedience to it, and is thus our indirect duty.

C. OF LOVE TO MEN

Love is a matter of feeling, not of will or volition, and I cannot love because I will to do so, still less because I ought (I cannot be necessitated to love); hence there is no such thing as a duty to love. Benevolence, however (amor benevolentiae), as a mode of action, may be subject to a law of duty. Disinterested benevolence is often called (though very improperly) love; even where the happiness of the other is not concerned, but the complete and free surrender of all one's own ends to the ends of another (even a superhuman) being, love is spoken of as being also our duty. But all duty is necessitation or constraint, although it may be self-constraint according to a law. But what is done from constraint is not done from love.

It is a duty to do good to other men according to our power, whether we love them or not, and this duty loses nothing of its weight, although we must make the sad remark that our species, alas! is not such as to be found particularly worthy of love when we know it more closely. Hatred of men, however, is always hateful: even though without any active hostility it consists only in complete aversion from mankind (the solitary misanthropy). For benevolence still remains a duty even towards the manhater, whom one cannot love, but to whom we can show kindness.

To hate vice in men is neither duty nor against duty, but a mere feeling of horror of vice, the will having no influence on the feeling nor the feeling on the will. Beneficence is a duty. He who often practises this, and sees his beneficent purpose succeed, comes at last really to love him whom he has benefited. When, therefore, it is said: "Thou shalt love thy neighbour as thyself," this does not mean, "Thou shalt first of all love, and by means of this love (in the next place) do him good"; but: "Do good to thy neighbour, and this beneficence will produce in thee the love of men (as a settled habit of inclination to beneficence)."

The love of complacency (amor complacentiae,) would therefore alone be direct. This is a pleasure immediately connected with the idea of the existence of an object, and to have a duty to this, that is, to be necessitated to find pleasure in a thing, is a contradiction.

D. OF RESPECT

Respect (reverentia) is likewise something merely subjective; a feeling of a peculiar kind not a judgement about an object which it would be a duty to effect or to advance. For if considered as duty it could only be conceived as such by means of the respect which we have for it. To have a duty to this, therefore, would be as much as to say to be bound in duty to have a duty. When, therefore, it is said: "Man has a duty of self-esteem," this is improperly stated, and we ought rather to say: "The law within him inevitably forces from him respect for his own being, and this feeling (which is of a peculiar kind) is a basis of certain duties, that is, of certain actions which may be consistent with his duty to himself." But we cannot say that he has a duty of respect for himself; for he must have respect for the law within himself, in order to be able to conceive duty at all.

XIII. General Principles of the Metaphysics of Morals in the treatment of Pure Ethics

First. A duty can have only a single ground of obligation; and if two or more proof of it are adduced, this is a certain mark that either no valid proof has yet been given, or that there are several distinct duties which have been regarded as one.

For all moral proofs, being philosophical, can only be drawn by means of rational knowledge from concepts, not like mathematics, through the construction of concepts. The latter science admits a variety of proofs of one and the same theorem; because in intuition a priori there may be several properties of an object, all of which lead back to the very same principle. If, for instance, to prove the duty of veracity, an argument is drawn first from the harm that a lie causes to other men; another from the worthlessness of a liar and the violation of his own self-respect, what is proved in the former argument is a duty of benevolence, not of veracity, that is to say, not the duty which required to be proved, but a different one. Now, if, in giving a variety of proof for one and the same theorem, we flatter ourselves that the multitude of reasons will compensate the lack of weight in each taken separately, this is a very unphilosophical resource, since it betrays trickery and dishonesty; for several insufficient proofs placed beside one another do not produce certainty, nor even probability. They should advance as reason and consequence in a series, up to the sufficient reason, and it is only in this way that they can have the force of proof. Yet the former is the usual device of the rhetorician.

Secondly. The difference between virtue and vice cannot be sought in the degree in which certain maxims are followed, but only in the specific quality of the maxims (their relation to the law). In other words, the vaunted principle of Aristotle, that virtue is the mean between two vices, is false. For instance, suppose that good management is given as the mean between two vices, prodigality and avarice; then its origin as a virtue can neither be defined as the gradual diminution of the former vice (by saving), nor as the increase of the expenses of the miserly. These vices, in fact, cannot be viewed as if they, proceeding as it were in opposite directions, met together in good management; but each of them has its own maxim, which necessarily contradicts that of the other.

For the same reason, no vice can be defined as an excess in the practice of certain actions beyond what is proper (e.g., Prodigalitas est excessus in consumendis opibus); or, as a less exercise of them than is fitting (Avaritia est defectus, etc.). For since in this way the degree is left quite undefined, and the question whether conduct accords with duty or not, turns wholly on this, such an account is of no use as a definition.

Thirdly. Ethical virtue must not be estimated by the power we attribute to man of fulfilling the law; but, conversely, the moral power must be estimated by the law, which commands categorically; not, therefore, by the empirical knowledge that we have of men as they are, but by the rational knowledge how, according to the ideas of humanity, they ought to be. These three maxims of the scientific treatment of ethics are opposed to the older apophthegms:

1. There is only one virtue and only one vice.

2. Virtue is the observance of the mean path between two opposite vices.

3. Virtue (like prudence) must be learned from experience.

XIV. Of Virtue in General

Virtue signifies a moral strength of will. But this does not exhaust the notion; for such strength might also belong to a holy (superhuman) being, in whom no opposing impulse counteracts the law of his rational will; who therefore willingly does everything in accordance with the law. Virtue then is the moral strength of a man's will in his obedience to duty; and this is a moral necessitation by his own law giving reason, inasmuch as this constitutes itself a power executing the law. It is not itself a duty, nor is it a duty to possess it (otherwise we should be in duty bound to have a duty), but it commands, and accompanies its command with a moral constraint (one possible by laws of internal freedom). But since this should be irresistible, strength is requisite, and the degree of this strength can be estimated only by the magnitude of the hindrances which man creates for himself, by his inclinations. Vices, the brood of unlawful dispositions, are the monsters that he has to combat; wherefore this moral strength as fortitude (fortitudo moralis) constitutes the greatest and only true martial glory of man; it is also called the true wisdom, namely, the practical, because it makes the ultimate end of the existence of man on earth its own end. Its possession alone makes man free, healthy, rich, a king, etc., nor either chance or fate deprive him of this, since he possesses himself, and the virtuous cannot lose his virtue.

All the encomiums bestowed on the ideal of humanity in its moral perfection can lose nothing of their practical reality by the examples of what men now are, have been, or will probably be hereafter; anthropology which proceeds from mere empirical knowledge cannot impair anthroponomy which is erected by the unconditionally legislating reason; and although virtue may now and then be called meritorious (in relation to men, not to the law), and be worthy of reward, yet in itself, as it is its own end, so also it must be regarded as its own reward.

Virtue considered in its complete perfection is, therefore, regarded not as if man possessed virtue, but as if virtue possessed the man, since in the former case it would appear as though he had still had the choice (for which he would then require another virtue, in order to select virtue from all other wares offered to him). To conceive a plurality of virtues (as we unavoidably must) is nothing else but to conceive various moral objects to which the (rational) will is led by the single principle of virtue; and it is the same with the opposite vices. The expression which personifies both is a contrivance for affecting the sensibility, pointing, however, to a moral sense. Hence it follows that an aesthetic of morals is not a part, but a subjective exposition of the Metaphysic of Morals; in which the emotions that accompany the force of the moral law make the that force to be felt; for example: disgust, horror, etc., which gives a sensible moral aversion in order to gain the precedence from the merely sensible incitement.

XV. Of the Principle on which Ethics is separated from

Jurisprudence

This separation on which the subdivision of moral philosophy in general rests, is founded on this: that the notion of freedom, which is common to both, makes it necessary to divide duties into those of external and those of internal freedom; the latter of which alone are ethical. Hence this internal freedom which is the condition of all ethical duty must be discussed as a preliminary (discursus praeliminaris), just as above the doctrine of conscience was discussed as the condition of all duty.

REMARKS

Of the Doctrine of Virtue on the Principle Of Internal Freedom.

Habit (habitus) is a facility of action and a subjective perfection of the elective will. But not every such facility is a free habit (habitus libertatis); for if it is custom (assuetudo), that is, a uniformity of action which, by frequent repetition, has become a necessity, then it is not a habit proceeding from freedom, and therefore not a moral habit. Virtue therefore cannot be defined as a habit of free law-abiding actions, unless indeed we add "determining itself in its action by the idea of the law"; and then this habit is not a property of the elective will, but of the rational will, which is a faculty that in adopting a rule also declares it to be a universal law, and it is only such a habit that can be reckoned as virtue. Two things are required for internal freedom: to be master of oneself in a given case (animus sui compos) and to have command over oneself (imperium in semetipsum), that is to subdue his emotions and to govern his passions. With these conditions, the character (indoles) is noble (erecta); in the opposite case, it is ignoble (indoles abjecta serva).

XVI. Virtue requires, first of all, Command over Oneself

Emotions and passions are essentially distinct; the former belong to feeling in so far as this coming before reflection makes it more difficult or even impossible. Hence emotion is called hasty (animus praeceps). And reason declares through the notion of virtue that a man should collect himself; but this weakness in the life of one's understanding, joined with the strength of a mental excitement, is only a lack of virtue (Untugend), and as it were a weak and childish thing, which may very well consist with the best will, and has further this one good thing in it, that this storm soon subsides. A propensity to emotion (e.g., resentment) is therefore not so closely related to vice as passion is. Passion, on the other hand, is the sensible appetite grown into a permanent inclination (e. g., hatred in contrast to resentment). The calmness with which one indulges it leaves room for reflection and allows the mind to frame principles thereon for itself; and thus when the inclination falls upon what contradicts the law, to brood on it, to allow it to root itself deeply, and thereby to take up evil (as of set purpose) into one's maxim; and this is then specifically evil, that is, it is a true vice.

Virtue, therefore, in so far as it is based on internal freedom, contains a positive command for man, namely, that he should bring all his powers and inclinations under his rule (that of reason); and this is a positive precept of command over himself which is additional to the prohibition, namely, that he should not allow himself to be governed by his feelings and inclinations (the duty of apathy); since, unless reason takes the reins of government into its own hands, the feelings and inclinations play the master over the man.

XVII. Virtue necessarily presupposes Apathy (considered as Strength)

This word (apathy) has come into bad repute, just as if it meant want of feeling, and therefore subjective indifference with respect to the objects of the elective will; it is supposed to be a weakness. This misconception may be avoided by giving the name moral apathy to that want of emotion which is to be distinguished from indifference. In the former, the feelings arising from sensible impressions lose their influence on the moral feeling only because the respect for the law is more powerful than all of them together. It is only the apparent strength of a fever patient that makes even the lively sympathy with good rise to an emotion, or rather degenerate into it. Such an emotion is called enthusiasm, and it is with reference to this that we are to explain the moderation which is usually recommended in virtuous practices:

Insani sapiens nomen ferat, aequus uniqui

Ultra quam satis est virtutem si petat ipsam.

For otherwise it is absurd to imagine that one could be too wise or too virtuous. The emotion always belongs to the sensibility, no matter by what sort of object it may be excited. The true strength of virtue is the mind at rest, with a firm, deliberate resolution to bring its law into practice. That is the state of health in the moral life; on the contrary, the emotion, even when it is excited by the idea of the good, is a momentary glitter which leaves exhaustion after it. We may apply the term fantastically virtuous to the man who will admit nothing to be indifferent in respect of morality (adiaphora), and who strews all his steps with duties, as with traps, and will not allow it to be indifferent whether a man eats fish or flesh, drink beer or wine, when both agree with him; a micrology which, if adopted into the doctrine of virtue, would make its rule a tyranny.

REMARK

Virtue is always in progress, and yet always begins from the beginning. The former follows from the fact that, objectively considered, it is an ideal and unattainable, and yet it is a duty constantly to approximate to it. The second is founded subjectively on the nature of man which is affected by inclinations, under the influence of which virtue, with its maxims adopted once for all, can never settle in a position of rest; but, if it is not rising, inevitably falls; because moral maxims cannot, like technical, be based on custom (for this belongs to the physical character of the determination of will); but even if the practice of them become a custom, the agent would thereby lose the freedom in the choice of his maxims, which freedom is the character of an action done from duty.

ON_CONSCIENCE

The consciousness of an internal tribunal in man (before which "his thoughts accuse or excuse one another") is CONSCIENCE.

Every man has a conscience, and finds himself observed by an inward judge which threatens and keeps him in awe (reverence combined with fear); and this power which watches over the laws within him is not something which he himself (arbitrarily) makes, but it is incorporated in his being. It follows him like his shadow, when he thinks to escape. He may indeed stupefy himself with pleasures and distractions, but cannot avoid now and then coming to himself or awaking, and then he at once perceives its awful voice. In his utmost depravity, he may, indeed, pay no attention to it, but he cannot avoid hearing it.

Now this original intellectual and (as a conception of duty) moral capacity, called conscience, has this peculiarity in it, that although its business is a business of man with himself, yet he finds himself compelled by his reason to transact it as if at the command of another person. For the transaction here is the conduct of a trial (causa) before a tribunal. But that he who is accused by his conscience should be conceived as one and the same person with the judge is an absurd conception of a judicial court; for then the complainant would always lose his case. Therefore, in all duties the conscience of the man must regard another than himself as the judge of his actions, if it is to avoid self-contradiction. Now this other may be an actual or a merely ideal person which reason frames to itself. Such an idealized person (the authorized judge of conscience) must be one who knows the heart; for the tribunal is set up in the inward part of man; at the same time he must also be all-obliging, that is, must be or be conceived as a person in respect of whom all duties are to be regarded as his commands; since conscience is the inward judge of all free actions. Now, since such a moral being must at the same time possess all power (in heaven and earth), since otherwise he could not give his commands their proper effect (which the office of judge necessarily requires), and since such a moral being possessing power over all is called GOD, hence conscience must be conceived as the subjective principle of a responsibility for one's deeds before God; nay, this latter concept is contained (though it be only obscurely) in every moral self-consciousness.

THE END

9 781835 915646

THE UNKNOWN MASTERPIECE

By Honoré De Balzac

I — GILLETTE

On a cold December morning in the year 1612, a young man, whose clothing was somewhat of the thinnest, was walking to and fro before a gateway in the Rue des Grands-Augustins in Paris. He went up and down the street before this house with the irresolution of a gallant who dares not venture into the presence of the mistress whom he loves for the first time, easy of access though she may be; but after a sufficiently long interval of hesitation, he at last crossed the threshold and inquired of an old woman, who was sweeping out a large room on the ground floor, whether Master Porbus was within. Receiving a reply in the affirmative, the young man went slowly up the staircase, like a gentleman but newly come to court, and doubtful as to his reception by the king. He came to a stand once more on the landing at the head of the stairs, and again he hesitated before raising his hand to the grotesque knocker on the door of the studio, where doubtless the painter was at work — Master Porbus, sometime painter in ordinary to Henri IV till Mary de' Medici took Rubens into favor.

The young man felt deeply stirred by an emotion that must thrill the hearts of all great artists when, in the pride of their youth and their first love of art, they come into the presence of a master or stand before a masterpiece. For all human sentiments there is a time of early blossoming, a day of generous enthusiasm that gradually fades until nothing is left of happiness but a memory, and glory is known for a delusion. Of all these delicate and short-lived emotions, none so resemble love as the passion of a young artist for his art, as he is about to enter on the blissful martyrdom of his career of glory and disaster, of vague expectations and real disappointments.

Those who have missed this experience in the early days of light purses; who have not, in the dawn of their genius, stood in the presence of a master and felt the throbbing of their hearts, will always carry in their inmost souls a chord that has never been touched, and in their work an indefinable quality will be lacking, a something in the stroke of the brush, a mysterious element that we call poetry. The swaggerers, so puffed up by self-conceit that they are confident over-soon of their success, can never be taken for men of talent save by fools. From this point of view, if youthful modesty is the measure of youthful genius, the stranger on the staircase might be allowed to have something in him; for he seemed to possess the indescribable diffidence, the early timidity that artists are bound to lose in the course of a great career, even as pretty women lose it as they make progress in the arts of coquetry. Self-distrust vanishes as triumph succeeds to triumph, and modesty is, perhaps, distrust of itself.

The poor neophyte was so overcome by the consciousness of his own presumption and insignificance, that it began to look as if he was hardly likely to penetrate into the studio of the painter, to whom we owe the wonderful portrait of Henri IV. But fate was propitious; an old man came up the staircase. From the quaint costume of this newcomer, his collar of magnificent lace, and a certain serene gravity in his bearing, the first arrival thought that this personage must be either a patron or a friend of the court painter. He stood aside therefore upon the landing to allow the visitor to pass, scrutinizing him curiously the while. Perhaps he might hope to find the good nature of an artist or to receive the good offices of an amateur not unfriendly to the arts; but besides an almost diabolical expression in the face that met his gaze, there was that indescribable something which has an irresistible attraction for artists.

Picture that face. A bald high forehead and rugged jutting brows above a small flat nose turned up at the end, as in the portraits of Socrates and Rabelais; deep lines about the mocking mouth; a short chin, carried proudly, covered with a grizzled pointed beard; sea-green eyes that age might seem to have dimmed were it not for the contrast between the iris and the surrounding mother-of-pearl tints, so that it seemed as if under the stress of anger or enthusiasm there would be a magnetic power to quell or kindle in their glances. The face was withered beyond wont by the fatigue of years, yet it seemed aged still more by the thoughts that had worn away both soul and body. There were no lashes to the deep-set eyes, and scarcely a trace of the arching lines of the eyebrows above them. Set this head on a spare and feeble frame, place it in a frame of lace wrought like an engraved silver fish-slice, imagine a heavy gold chain over the old man's black doublet, and you will have some dim idea of this strange personage, who seemed still more fantastic in the sombre twilight of the staircase. One of Rembrandt's portraits might have stepped down from its frame to walk in an appropriate atmosphere of gloom, such as the great painter loved. The older man gave the younger a shrewd glance, and knocked thrice at the door. It was opened by a man of forty or thereabout, who seemed to be an invalid.

"Good day, Master."

Porbus bowed respectfully, and held the door open for the younger man to enter, thinking that the latter accompanied his visitor; and when he saw that the neophyte stood a while as if spellbound, feeling, as every artist-nature must feel, the fascinating influence of the first sight of a studio in which the material processes of art are revealed, Porbus troubled himself no more about this second comer.

All the light in the studio came from a window in the roof, and was concentrated upon an easel, where a canvas stood untouched as yet save for three or four outlines in chalk. The daylight scarcely reached the remoter angles and corners of the vast room; they were as dark as night, but the silver ornamented breastplate of a Reiter's corselet, that hung upon the wall, attracted a stray gleam to its dim abiding-place among the brown shadows; or a shaft of light shot across the carved and glistening surface of an antique sideboard covered with curious silver-plate, or struck out a line of glittering dots among the raised threads of the golden warp of some old brocaded curtains, where the lines of the stiff, heavy folds were broken, as the stuff had been flung carelessly down to serve as a model.

Plaster *écorchés* stood about the room; and here and there, on shelves and tables, lay fragments of classical sculpture-torsos of antique goddesses, worn smooth as though all the years of the centuries that had passed over them had been lovers' kisses. The walls were covered, from floor to ceiling, with countless sketches in charcoal, red chalk, or pen and ink. Amid the litter and confusion of color boxes, overturned stools, flasks of oil, and essences, there was just room to move so as to reach the illuminated circular space where the easel stood. The light from the window in the roof fell full upon Por-bus's pale face and on the ivory-tinted forehead of his strange visitor. But in another moment the younger man heeded nothing but a picture that had already become famous even in those stormy days of political and religious revolution, a picture that a few of the zealous worshipers, who have so often kept the sacred fire of art alive in evil days, were wont to go on pilgrimage to see. The beautiful panel represented a Saint Mary of Egypt about to pay her passage across the seas. It was a masterpiece destined for Mary de' Medici, who sold it in later years of poverty.

"I like your saint," the old man remarked, addressing Porbus. "I would give you ten golden crowns for her over and above the price the Queen is paying; but as for putting a spoke in that wheel, — the devil take it!"

"It is good then?"

"Hey! hey!" said the old man; "good, say you? — Yes and no. Your good woman is not badly done, but she is not alive. You artists fancy that when a figure is correctly drawn, and everything in its place according to the rules of anatomy, there is nothing more to be done. You make up the flesh tints beforehand on your palettes according to your formulae, and fill in the outlines with due care that one side of the face shall be darker than the other; and because you look from time to time at a naked woman who stands on the platform before you, you fondly imagine that you have copied nature, think yourselves to be painters, believe that you have wrested His secret from God. Pshaw! You may know your syntax thoroughly and make no blunders in your grammar, but it takes that and something more to make a great poet. Look at your saint, Porbus! At a first glance she is admirable; look at her again, and you see at once that she is glued to the background, and that you could not walk round her. She is a silhouette that turns but one side of her face to all beholders, a figure cut out of canvas, an image with no power to move nor change her position. I feel as if there were no air between that arm and the background, no space, no sense of distance in your canvas. The perspective is perfectly correct, the strength of the coloring is accurately diminished with the distance; but, in spite of these praiseworthy efforts, I could never bring myself to believe that the warm breath of life comes and goes in that beautiful body. It seems to me that if I laid my hand on the firm, rounded throat, it would be cold as marble to the touch. No, my friend, the blood does not flow beneath that ivory skin, the tide of life does not flush those delicate fibres, the purple veins that trace a network beneath the transparent amber of her brow and breast. Here the pulse seems to beat, there it is motionless, life and death are at strife in every detail; here you see a woman, there a statue, there again a corpse. Your creation is incomplete. You had only power to breathe a portion of your soul into your beloved work. The fire of Prometheus died out again and again in your hands; many a spot in your picture has not been touched by the divine flame."

"But how is it, dear master?" Porbus asked respectfully, while the young man with difficulty repressed his strong desire to beat the critic.

"Ah!" said the old man, "it is this! You have halted between two manners. You have hesitated between drawing and color, between the dogged attention to detail, the stiff precision of the German masters and the dazzling glow, the joyous exuberance of Italian painters. You have set yourself to imitate Hans Holbein and Titian, Albrecht Durer and Paul Veronese in a single picture. A magnificent ambition truly, but what has come of it? Your work has neither the severe charm of a dry execution nor the magical illusion of Italian *chiaroscuro*. Titian's rich golden coloring poured into Albrecht Dureras austere outlines has shattered them, like molten bronze bursting through the mold that is not strong enough to hold it. In other places the outlines have held firm, imprisoning and obscuring the magnificent, glowing flood of Venetian color. The drawing of the face is not perfect, the coloring is not perfect; traces of that unlucky indecision are to be seen everywhere. Unless you felt strong enough to fuse the two opposed manners in the fire of your own genius, you should have cast in your lot boldly with the one or the other, and so have obtained the unity which simulates one of the conditions of life itself. Your work is only true in the centres; your outlines are false, they project nothing, there is no hint of anything behind them. There is truth here," said the old man, pointing to the breast of the Saint, "and again here," he went on, indicating the rounded shoulder. "But there," once more returning to the column of the throat, "everything is false. Let us go no further into detail, you would be disheartened."

The old man sat down on a stool, and remained a while without speaking, with his face buried in his hands.

"Yet I studied that throat from the life, dear master," Porbus began; "it happens sometimes, for our misfortune, that real effects in nature look improbable when transferred to canvas —"

"The aim of art is not to copy nature, but to express it. You are not a servile copyist, but a poet!" cried the old man sharply, cutting Porbus short with an imperious gesture. "Otherwise a sculptor might make a plaster cast of a living woman and save himself all further trouble. Well, try to make a cast of your mistress's hand, and set up the thing before you. You will see a monstrosity, a dead mass, bearing no resemblance to the living hand; you would be compelled to have recourse to the chisel of a sculptor who, without making an exact copy, would represent for you its movement and its life. We must detect the spirit, the informing soul in the appearances of things and beings. Effects! What are effects but the accidents of life, not life itself? A hand, since I have taken that example, is not only a part of a body, it is the expression and extension of a thought that must be grasped and rendered. Neither painter nor poet nor sculptor may separate the effect from the cause, which are inevitably contained the one in the other. There begins the real struggle! Many a painter achieves success instinctively, unconscious of the task that is set before art. You draw a woman, yet you do not see her! Not so do you succeed in wresting Nature's secrets from her! You are reproducing mechanically the model that you copied in your master's studio. You do not penetrate far enough into the inmost secrets of the mystery of form; you do not seek with love enough and perseverance enough after the form that baffles and eludes you. Beauty is a thing severe and unapproachable, never to be won by a languid lover. You must lie in wait for her coming and take her unawares, press her hard and clasp her in a tight embrace, and force her to yield. Form is a Proteus more intangible and more manifold than the Proteus of the legend; compelled, only after long wrestling, to stand forth manifest in his true aspect. Some of you are satisfied with the first shape, or at most by the second or the third that appears. Not thus wrestle the victors, the unvanquished painters who never suffer themselves to be deluded by all those treacherous shadow-shapes; they persevere till Nature at the last stands bare to their gaze, and her very soul is revealed.

"In this manner worked Rafael," said the old man, taking off his cap to express his reverence for the King of Art. "His transcendent greatness came of the intimate sense that, in him, seems as if it would shatter external form. Form in his figures (as with us) is a symbol, a means of communicating sensations, ideas, the vast imaginings of a poet. Every face is a whole world. The subject of the portrait appeared for him bathed in the light of a divine vision; it was revealed by an inner voice, the finger of God laid bare the sources of expression in the past of a whole life.

"You clothe your women in fair raiment of flesh, in gracious veiling of hair; but where is the blood, the source of passion and of calm, the cause of the particular effect? Why, this brown Egyptian of yours, my good Porbus, is a colorless creature! These figures that you set before us are painted bloodless fantoms; and you call that painting, you call that art!

"Because you have made something more like a woman than a house, you think that you have set your fingers on the goal; you are quite proud that you need not to write *currus venustus* or *pulcher homo* beside your figures, as early painters were wont to do and you fancy that you have done wonders. Ah! my good friend, there is still something more to learn, and you will use up a great deal of chalk and cover many a canvas before you will learn it. Yes, truly, a woman carries her head in just such a way, so she holds her garments gathered into her hand; her eyes grow dreamy and soft with that expression of meek sweetness, and even so the quivering shadow of the lashes hovers upon her cheeks. It is all there, and yet it is not there. What is lacking? A nothing, but that nothing is everything.

"There you have the semblance of life, but you do not express its fulness and effluence, that indescribable something, perhaps the soul itself, that envelopes the outlines of the body like a haze; that flower of life, in short, that Titian and Rafael caught. Your utmost achievement hitherto has only brought you to the starting-point. You might now perhaps begin to do excellent work, but you grow weary all too soon; and the crowd admires, and those who know smile.

"Oh, Mabuse! oh, my master!" cried the strange speaker, "thou art a thief! Thou hast carried away the secret of life with thee!"

"Nevertheless," he began again, "this picture of yours is worth more than all the paintings of that rascal Rubens, with his mountains of Flemish flesh raddled with vermilion, his torrents of red hair, his riot of color. You, at least have color there, and feeling and drawing—the three essentials in art."

The young man roused himself from his deep musings.

"Why, my good man, the Saint is sublime!" he cried. "There is a subtlety of imagination about those two figures, the Saint Mary and the Shipman, that can not be found among Italian masters; I do not know a single one of them capable of imagining the Shipman's hesitation."

"Did that little malapert come with you?" asked Porbus of the older man.

"Alas! master, pardon my boldness," cried the neophyte, and the color mounted to his face. "I am unknown—a dauber by instinct, and but lately come to this city—the fountain-head of all learning."

"Set to work," said Porbus, handing him a bit of red chalk and a sheet of paper.

The new-comer quickly sketched the Saint Mary line for line.

"Aha!" exclaimed the old man. "Your name?" he added.

The young man wrote "Nicolas Poussin" below the sketch.

"Not bad that for a beginning," said the strange speaker, who had discoursed so wildly. "I see that we can talk of art in your presence. I do not blame you for admiring Porbus's saint. In the eyes of the world she is a masterpiece, and those alone who have been initiated into the inmost mysteries of art can discover her shortcomings. But it is worth while to give you the lesson, for you are able to understand it, so I will show you how little it needs to complete this picture. You must be all eyes, all attention, for it may be that such a chance of learning will never come in your way again—Porbus! your palette."

Porbus went in search of palette and brushes. The little old man turned back his sleeves with impatient energy, seized the palette, covered with many hues, that Porbus handed to him, and snatched rather than took a handful of brushes of various sizes from the hands of his acquaintance. His pointed beard suddenly bristled—a menacing movement that expressed the prick of a lover's fancy. As he loaded his brush, he muttered between his teeth, "These paints are only fit to fling out of the window, together with the fellow who ground them, their crudeness and falseness are disgusting! How can one paint with this?"

He dipped the tip of the brush with feverish eagerness in the different pigments, making the circuit of the palette several times more quickly than the organist of a cathedral sweeps the octaves on the keyboard of his clavier for the "O Filii" at Easter.

Porbus and Poussin, on either side of the easel, stood stock-still, watching with intense interest.

"Look, young man," he began again, "see how three or four strokes of the brush and a thin glaze of blue let in the free air to play about the head of the poor Saint, who must have felt stifled and oppressed by the close atmosphere! See how the drapery begins to flutter; you feel that it is lifted by the breeze! A moment ago it hung as heavily and stiffly as if it were held out by pins. Do you see how the satin sheen that I have just given to the breast rends the pliant, silken softness of a young girl's skin, and how the brown-red, blended with burnt ochre, brings warmth into the cold gray of the deep shadow where the blood lay congealed instead of coursing through the veins? Young man, young man, no master could teach you how to do this that I am doing before your eyes. Mabuse alone possessed the secret of giving life to his figures; Mabuse had but one pupil—that was I. I have had none, and I am old. You have sufficient intelligence to imagine the rest from the glimpses that I am giving you."

While the old man was speaking, he gave a touch here and there; sometimes two strokes of the brush, sometimes a single one; but every stroke told so well, that the whole picture seemed transfigured — the painting was flooded with light. He worked with such passionate fervor that beads of sweat gathered upon his bare forehead; he worked so quickly, in brief, impatient jerks, that it seemed to young Poussin as if some familiar spirit inhabiting the body of this strange being took a grotesque pleasure in making use of the man's hands against his own will. The unearthly glitter of his eyes, the convulsive movements that seemed like struggles, gave to this fancy a semblance of truth which could not but stir a young imagination. The old man continued, saying as he did so —

"Paf! paf! that is how to lay it on, young man! — Little touches! come and bring a glow into those icy cold tones for me! Just so! Pon! pon! pon!" and those parts of the picture that he had pointed out as cold and lifeless flushed with warmer hues, a few bold strokes of color brought all the tones of the picture into the required harmony with the glowing tints of the Egyptian, and the differences in temperament vanished.

"Look you, youngster, the last touches make the picture. Porbus has given it a hundred strokes for every one of mine. No one thanks us for what lies beneath. Bear that in mind."

At last the restless spirit stopped, and turning to Porbus and Poussin, who were speechless with admiration, he spoke —

"This is not as good as my 'Belle Noiseuse'; still one might put one's name to such a thing as this. — Yes, I would put my name to it," he added, rising to reach for a mirror, in which he looked at the picture. — "And now," he said, "will you both come and breakfast with me? I have a smoked ham and some very fair wine!... Eh! eh! the times may be bad, but we can still have some talk about art! We can talk like equals.... Here is a little fellow who has aptitude," he added, laying a hand on Nicolas Poussin's shoulder.

In this way the stranger became aware of the threadbare condition of the Norman's doublet. He drew a leather purse from his girdle, felt in it, found two gold coins, and held them out.

"I will buy your sketch," he said.

"Take it," said Porbus, as he saw the other start and flush with embarrassment, for Poussin had the pride of poverty. "Pray, take it; he has a couple of king's ransoms in his pouch!"

The three came down together from the studio, and, talking of art by the way, reached a picturesque wooden house hard by the Pont Saint-Michel. Poussin wondered a moment at its ornament, at the knocker, at the frames of the casements, at the scroll-work designs, and in the next he stood in a vast low-ceiled room. A table, covered with tempting dishes, stood near the blazing fire, and (luck unhoped for) he was in the company of two great artists full of genial good humor.

"Do not look too long at that canvas, young man," said Porbus, when he saw that Poussin was standing, struck with wonder, before a painting. "You would fall a victim to despair."

It was the "Adam" painted by Mabuse to purchase his release from the prison, where his creditors had so long kept him. And, as a matter of fact, the figure stood out so boldly and convincingly, that Nicolas Poussin began to understand the real meaning of the words poured out by the old artist, who was himself looking at the picture with apparent satisfaction, but without enthusiasm. "I have done better than that!" he seemed to be saying to himself.

"There is life in it," he said aloud; "in that respect my poor master here surpassed himself, but there is some lack of truth in the background. The man lives indeed; he is rising, and will come toward us; but the atmosphere, the sky, the air, the breath of the breeze—you look and feel for them, but they are not there. And then the man himself is, after all, only a man! Ah! but the one man in the world who came direct from the hands of God must have had a something divine about him that is wanting here. Mabuse himself would grind his teeth and say so when he was not drunk."

Poussin looked from the speaker to Porbus, and from Porbus to the speaker, with restless curiosity. He went up to the latter to ask for the name of their host; but the painter laid a finger on his lips with an air of mystery. The young man's interest was excited; he kept silence, but hoped that sooner or later some word might be let fall that would reveal the name of his entertainer. It was evident that he was a man of talent and very wealthy, for Porbus listened to him respectfully, and the vast room was crowded with marvels of art.

A magnificent portrait of a woman, hung against the dark oak panels of the wall, next caught Poussin's attention.

"What a glorious Giorgione!" he cried.

"No," said his host, "it is an early daub of mine—"

"Gramercy! I am in the abode of the god of painting, it seems!" cried Poussin ingenuously.

The old man smiled as if he had long grown familiar with such praise.

"Master Frenhofer!" said Porbus, "do you think you could spare me a little of your capital Rhine wine?"

"A couple of pipes!" answered his host; "one to discharge a debt, for the pleasure of seeing your pretty sinner, the other as a present from a friend."

"Ah! if I had my health," returned Porbus, "and if you would but let me see your 'Belle Noiseuse,' I would paint some great picture, with breadth in it and depth; the figures should be life-size."

"Let you see my work!" cried the painter in agitation. "No, no! it is not perfect yet; something still remains for me to do. Yesterday, in the dusk," he said, "I thought I had reached the end. Her eyes seemed moist, the flesh quivered, something stirred the tresses of her hair. She breathed! But though I have succeeded in reproducing Nature's roundness and relief on the flat surface of the canvas, this morning, by daylight, I found out my mistake. Ah! to achieve that glorious result I have studied the works of the great masters of color, stripping off coat after coat of color from Titian's canvas, analyzing the pigments of the king of light. Like that sovereign painter, I began the face in a slight tone with a supple and fat paste—for shadow is but an accident; bear that in mind, youngster!—Then I began afresh, and by half-tones and thin glazes of color less and less transparent, I gradually deepened the tints to the deepest black of the strongest shadows. An ordinary painter makes his shadows something entirely different in nature from the high lights; they are wood or brass, or what you will, anything but flesh in shadow. You feel that even if those figures were to alter their position, those shadow stains would never be cleansed away, those parts of the picture would never glow with light.

"I have escaped one mistake, into which the most famous painters have sometimes fallen; in my canvas the whiteness shines through the densest and most persistent shadow. I have not marked out the limits of my figure in hard, dry outlines, and brought every least anatomical detail into prominence (like a host of dunces, who fancy that they can draw because they can trace a line elaborately smooth and clean), for the human body is not contained within the limits of line. In this the sculptor can approach the truth more nearly than we painters. Nature's way is a complicated succession of curve within curve. Strictly speaking, there is no such thing as drawing. — Do not laugh, young man; strange as that speech may seem to you, you will understand the truth in it some day. — A line is a method of expressing the effect of light upon an object; but there are no lines in Nature, everything is solid. We draw by modeling, that is to say, that we disengage an object from its setting; the distribution of the light alone gives to a body the appearance by which we know it. So I have not defined the outlines; I have suffused them with a haze of half-tints warm or golden, in such a sort that you can not lay your finger on the exact spot where background and contours meet. Seen from near, the picture looks a blur; it seems to lack definition; but step back two paces, and the whole thing becomes clear, distinct, and solid; the body stands out; the rounded form comes into relief; you feel that the air plays round it. And yet — I am not satisfied; I have misgivings. Perhaps one ought not to draw a single line; perhaps it would be better to attack the face from the centre, taking the highest prominences first, proceeding from them through the whole range of shadows to the heaviest of all. Is not this the method of the sun, the divine painter of the world? Oh, Nature, Nature! who has surprised thee, fugitive? But, after all, too much knowledge, like ignorance, brings you to a negation. I have doubts about my work."

There was a pause. Then the old man spoke again. "I have been at work upon it for ten years, young man; but what are ten short years in a struggle with Nature? Do we know how long Sir Pygmalion wrought at the one statue that came to life?" The old man fell into deep musings, and gazed before him with unseeing eyes, while he played unheedingly with his knife.

"Look, he is in conversation with his *domon!*" murmured Porbus.

At the word, Nicolas Poussin felt himself carried away by an unaccountable accession of artist's curiosity. For him the old man, at once intent and inert, the seer with the unseeing eyes, became something more than a man—a fantastic spirit living in a mysterious world, and countless vague thoughts awoke within his soul. The effect of this species of fascination upon his mind can no more be described in words than the passionate longing awakened in an exile's heart by the song that recalls his home. He thought of the scorn that the old man affected to display for the noblest efforts of art, of his wealth, his manners, of the deference paid to him by Porbus. The mysterious picture, the work of patience on which he had wrought so long in secret, was doubtless a work of genius, for the head of the Virgin which young Poussin had admired so frankly was beautiful even beside Mabuse's "Adam"—there was no mistaking the imperial manner of one of the princes of art. Everything combined to set the old man beyond the limits of human nature.

Out of the wealth of fancies in Nicolas Poussin's brain an idea grew, and gathered shape and clearness. He saw in this supernatural being a complete type of the artist nature, a nature mocking and kindly, barren and prolific, an erratic spirit intrusted with great and manifold powers which she too often abuses, leading sober reason, the Philistine, and sometimes even the amateur forth into a stony wilderness where they see nothing; but the white-winged maiden herself, wild as her fancies may be, finds epics there and castles and works of art. For Poussin, the enthusiast, the old man, was suddenly transfigured, and became Art incarnate, Art with its mysteries, its vehement passion and its dreams.

"Yes, my dear Porbus," Frenhofer continued, "hitherto I have never found a flawless model, a body with outlines of perfect beauty, the carnations — Ah! where does she live?" he cried, breaking in upon himself, "the undiscoverable Venus of the older time, for whom we have sought so often, only to find the scattered gleams of her beauty here and there? Oh! to behold once and for one moment, Nature grown perfect and divine, the Ideal at last, I would give all that I possess.... Nay, Beauty divine, I would go to seek thee in the dim land of the dead; like Orpheus, I would go down into the Hades of Art to bring back the life of art from among the shadows of death."

"We can go now," said Porbus to Poussin. "He neither hears nor sees us any longer."

"Let us go to his studio," said young Poussin, wondering greatly.

"Oh! the old fox takes care that no one shall enter it. His treasures are so carefully guarded that it is impossible for us to come at them. I have not waited for your suggestion and your fancy to attempt to lay hands on this mystery by force."

"So there is a mystery?" "Yes," answered Porbus. "Old Frenhofer is the only pupil Mabuse would take. Frenhofer became the painter's friend, deliverer, and father; he sacrificed the greater part of his fortune to enable Mabuse to indulge in riotous extravagance, and in return Mabuse bequeathed to him the secret of relief, the power of giving to his figures the wonderful life, the flower of Nature, the eternal despair of art, the secret which Ma-buse knew so well that one day when he had sold the flowered brocade suit in which he should have appeared at the Entry of Charles V, he accompanied his master in a suit of paper painted to resemble the brocade. The peculiar richness and splendor of the stuff struck the Emperor; he complimented the old drunkard's patron on the artist's appearance, and so the trick was brought to light. Frenhofer is a passionate enthusiast, who sees above and beyond other painters. He has meditated profoundly on color, and the absolute truth of line; but by the way of much research he has come to doubt the very existence of the objects of his search. He says, in moments of despondency, that there is no such thing as drawing, and that by means of lines we can only reproduce geometrical figures; but that is overshooting the mark, for by outline and shadow you can reproduce form without any color at all, which shows that our art, like Nature, is composed of an infinite number of elements. Drawing gives you the skeleton, the anatomical frame-' work, and color puts the life into it; but life without the skeleton is even more incomplete than a skeleton without life. But there is something else truer still, and it is this—f or painters, practise and observation are everything; and when theories and poetical ideas begin to quarrel with the brushes, the end is doubt, as has happened with our good friend, who is half crack-brained enthusiast, half painter. A sublime painter! but unlucky for him, he was born to riches, and so he has leisure to follow his fancies. Do not you follow his example! Work! painters have no business to think, except brush in hand."

"We will find a way into his studio!" cried Poussin confidently. He had ceased to heed Porbus's remarks. The other smiled at the young painter's enthusiasm, asked him to come to see him again, and they parted. Nicolas Poussin went slowly back to the Rue de la Harpe, and passed the modest hostelry where he was lodging without noticing it. A feeling of uneasiness prompted him to hurry up the crazy staircase till he reached a room at the top, a quaint, airy recess under the steep, high-pitched roof common among houses in old Paris. In the one dingy window of the place sat a young girl, who sprang up at once when she heard some one at the door; it was the prompting of love; she had recognized the painter's touch on the latch.

"What is the matter with you?" she asked.

"The matter is... is... Oh! I have felt that I am a painter! Until to-day I have had doubts, but now I believe in myself! There is the making of a great man in me! Never mind, Gillette, we shall be rich and happy! There is gold at the tips of those brushes—"

He broke off suddenly. The joy faded from his powerful and earnest face as he compared his vast hopes with his slender resources. The walls were covered with sketches in chalk on sheets of common paper. There were but four canvases in the room. Colors were very costly, and the young painter's palette was almost bare. Yet in the midst of his poverty he possessed and was conscious of the possession of inexhaustible treasures of the heart, of a devouring genius equal to all the tasks that lay before him.

He had been brought to Paris by a nobleman among his friends, or perchance by the consciousness of his powers; and in Paris he had found a mistress, one of those noble and generous souls who choose to suffer by a great man's side, who share his struggles and strive to understand his fancies, accepting their lot of poverty and love as bravely and dauntlessly as other women will set themselves to bear the burden of riches and make a parade of their insensibility. The smile that stole over Gillette's lips filled the garret with golden light, and rivaled the brightness of the sun in heaven. The sun, moreover, does not always shine in heaven, whereas Gillette was always in the garret, absorbed in her passion, occupied by Poussin's happiness and sorrow, consoling the genius which found an outlet in love before art engrossed it.

"Listen, Gillette. Come here."

The girl obeyed joyously, and sprang upon the painter's knee. Hers was perfect grace and beauty, and the loveliness of spring; she was adorned with all luxuriant fairness of outward form, lighted up by the glow of a fair soul within.

"Oh! God," he cried; "I shall never dare to tell her — "

"A secret?" she cried; "I must know it!"

Poussin was absorbed in his dreams.

"Do tell it me!"

"Gillette... poor beloved heart!..."

"Oh! do you want something of me?"

"Yes."

"If you wish me to sit once more for you as I did the other day," she continued with playful petulance, "I will never consent to do such a thing again, for your eyes say nothing all the while. You do not think of me at all, and yet you look at me — "

"Would you rather have me draw another woman?"

"Perhaps—if she were very ugly," she said.

"Well," said Poussin gravely, "and if, for the sake of my fame to come, if to make me a great painter, you must sit to some one else?"

"You may try me," she said; "you know quite well that I would not."

Poussin's head sank on her breast; he seemed to be overpowered by some intolerable joy or sorrow.

"Listen," she cried, plucking at the sleeve of Poussin's threadbare doublet, "I told you, Nick, that I would lay down my life for you; but I never promised you that I in my lifetime would lay down my love."

"Your love?" cried the young artist.

"If I showed myself thus to another, you would love me no longer, and I should feel myself unworthy of you. Obedience to your fancies was a natural and simple thing, was it not? Even against my own will, I am glad and even proud to do thy dear will. But for another, out upon it!"

"Forgive me, my Gillette," said the painter, falling upon his knees; "I would rather be beloved than famous. You are fairer than success and honors. There, fling the pencils away, and burn these sketches! I have made a mistake. I was meant to love and not to paint. Perish art and all its secrets!"

Gillette looked admiringly at him, in an ecstasy of happiness! She was triumphant; she felt instinctively that art was laid aside for her sake, and flung like a grain of incense at her feet.

"Yet he is only an old man," Poussin continued; "for him you would be a woman, and nothing more. You—so perfect!"

"I must love you indeed!" she cried, ready to sacrifice even love's scruples to the lover who had given up so much for her sake; "but I should bring about my own ruin. Ah! to ruin myself, to lose everything for you!... It is a very glorious thought! Ah! but you will forget me. Oh I what evil thought is this that has come to you?"

"I love you, and yet I thought of it," he said, with something like remorse, "Am I so base a wretch?"

"Let us consult Père Hardouin," she said.

"No, no! Let it be a secret between us."

"Very well; I will do it. But you must not be there," she said. "Stay at the door with your dagger in your hand; and if I call, rush in and kill the painter."

Poussin forgot everything but art. He held Gillette tightly in his arms.

"He loves me no longer!" thought Gillette when she was alone. She repented of her resolution already.

But to these misgivings there soon succeeded a sharper pain, and she strove to banish a hideous thought that arose in her own heart. It seemed to her that her own love had grown less already, with a vague suspicion that the painter had fallen somewhat in her eyes.

II—CATHERINE LESCAULT

Three months after Poussin and Porbus met, the latter went to see Master Frenhofer. The old man had fallen a victim to one of those profound and spontaneous fits of discouragement that are caused, according to medical logicians, by indigestion, flatulence, fever, or enlargement of the spleen; or, if you take the opinion of the Spiritualists, by the imperfections of our mortal nature. The good man had simply overworked himself in putting the finishing touches to his mysterious picture. He was lounging in a huge carved oak chair, covered with black leather, and did not change his listless attitude, but glanced at Porbus like a man who has settled down into low spirits.

"Well, master," said Porbus, "was the ultramarine bad that you sent for to Bruges? Is the new white difficult to grind? Is the oil poor, or are the brushes recalcitrant?"

"Alas!" cried the old man, "for a moment I thought that my work was finished, but I am sure that I am mistaken in certain details, and I can not rest until I have cleared my doubts. I am thinking of traveling. I am going to Turkey, to Greece, to Asia, in quest of a model, so as to compare my picture with the different living forms of Nature. Perhaps," and a smile of contentment stole over his face, "perhaps I have Nature herself up there. At times I am half afraid that a breath may waken her, and that she will escape me."

He rose to his feet as if to set out at once.

"Aha!" said Porbus, "I have come just in time to save you the trouble and expense of a journey."

"What?" asked Frenhofer in amazement.

"Young Poussin is loved by a woman of incomparable and flawless beauty. But, dear master, if he consents to lend her to you, at the least you ought to let us see your work."

The old man stood motionless and completely dazed.

"What!" he cried piteously at last, "show you my creation, my bride? Rend the veil that has kept my happiness sacred? It would be an infamous profanation. For ten years I have lived with her; she is mine, mine alone; she loves me. Has she not smiled at me, at each stroke of the brush upon the canvas? She has a soul—the soul that I have given her. She would blush if any eyes but mine should rest on her. To exhibit her! Where is the husband, the lover so vile as to bring the woman he loves to dishonor? When you paint a picture for the court, you do not put your whole soul into it; to courtiers you sell lay figures duly colored. My painting is no painting, it is a sentiment, a passion. She was born in my studio, there she must dwell in maiden solitude, and only when clad can she issue thence. Poetry and women only lay the last veil aside for their lovers Have we Rafael's model, Ariosto's Angelica, Dante's Beatrice? Nay, only their form and semblance. But this picture, locked away above in my studio, is an exception in our art. It is not a canvas, it is a woman—a woman with whom I talk. I share her thoughts, her tears, her laughter. Would you have me fling aside these ten years of happiness like a cloak? Would you have me cease at once to be father, lover, and creator? She is not a creature, but a creation.

"Bring your young painter here. I will give him my treasures; I will give him pictures by Correggio and Michelangelo and Titian; I will kiss his footprints in the dust; but make him my rival! Shame on me. Ah! ah! I am a lover first, and then a painter. Yes, with my latest sigh I could find strength to burn my 'Belle Noiseuse'; but—compel her to endure the gaze of a stranger, a young man and a painter!— Ah! no, no! I would kill him on the morrow who should sully her with a glance! Nay, you, my friend, I would kill you with my own hands in a moment if you did not kneel in reverence before her! Now, will you have me submit my idol to the careless eyes and senseless criticisms of fools? Ah! love is a mystery; it can only live hidden in the depths of the heart. You say, even to your friend, 'Behold her whom I love,' and there is an end of love."

The old man seemed to have grown young again; there was light and life in his eyes, and a faint flush of red in his pale face. His hands shook. Porbus was so amazed by the passionate vehemence of Frenhofer's words that he knew not what to reply to this utterance of an emotion as strange as it was profound. Was Frenhofer sane or mad? Had he fallen a victim to some freak of the artist's fancy? or were these ideas of his produced by the strange lightheadedness which comes over us during the long travail of a work of art. Would it be possible to come to terms with this singular passion?

Harassed by all these doubts, Porbus spoke—"Is it not woman for woman?" he said. "Does not Poussin submit his mistress to your gaze?"

"What is she?" retorted the other. "A mistress who will be false to him sooner or later. Mine will be faithful to me forever."

"Well, well," said Porbus, "let us say no more about it. But you may die before you will find such a flawless beauty as hers, even in Asia, and then your picture will be left unfinished.

"Oh! it is finished," said Frenhof er. "Standing before it you would think that it was a living woman lying on the velvet couch beneath the shadow of the curtains. Perfumes are burning on a golden tripod by her side. You would be tempted to lay your hand upon the tassel of the cord that holds back the curtains; it would seem to you that you saw her breast rise and fall as she breathed; that you beheld the living Catherine Lescault, the beautiful courtezan whom men called 'La Belle Noiseuse.' And yet—if I could but be sure—"

"Then go to Asia," returned Porbus, noticing a certain indecision in Frenhofer's face. And with that Porbus made a few steps toward the door. By that time Gillette and Nicolas Poussin had reached Frenhofer's house. The girl drew away her arm from her lover's as she stood on the threshold, and shrank back as if some presentiment flashed through her mind.

"Oh! what have I come to do here?" she asked of her lover in low vibrating tones, with her eyes fixed on his.

"Gillette, I have left you to decide; I am ready to obey you in everything. You are my conscience and my glory. Go home again; I shall be happier, perhaps, if you do not—"

"Am I my own when you speak to me like that? No, no; I am a child.—Come," she added, seemingly with a violent effort; "if our love dies, if I plant a long regret in my heart, your fame will be the reward of my obedience to your wishes, will it not? Let us go in. I shall still live on as a memory on your palette; that shall be life for me afterward."

The door opened, and the two lovers encountered Porbus, who was surprised by the beauty of Gillette, whose eyes were full of tears. He hurried her, trembling from head to foot, into the presence of the old painter.

"Here!" he cried, "is she not worth all the masterpieces in the world!"

Frenhofer trembled. There stood Gillette in the artless and childlike attitude of some timid and innocent Georgian, carried off by brigands, and confronted with a slave merchant. A shamefaced red flushed her face, her eyes drooped, her hands hung by her side, her strength seemed to have failed her, her tears protested against this outrage. Poussin cursed himself in despair that he should have brought his fair treasure from its hiding-place. The lover overcame the artist, and countless doubts assailed Poussin's heart when he saw youth dawn in the old man's eyes, as, like a painter, he discerned every line of the form hidden beneath the young girl's vesture. Then the lover's savage jealousy awoke.

"Gillette!" he cried, "let us go."

The girl turned joyously at the cry and the tone in which it was uttered, raised her eyes to his, looked at him, and fled to his arms.

"Ah! then you love me," she cried; "you love me!" and she burst into tears.

She had spirit enough to suffer in silence, but she had no strength to hide her joy.

"Oh! leave her with me for one moment," said the old painter, "and you shall compare her with my Catherine... yes — I consent."

Frenhofer's words likewise came from him like a lover's cry. His vanity seemed to be engaged for his semblance of womanhood; he anticipated the triumph of the beauty of his own creation over the beauty of the living girl.

"Do not give him time to change his mind!" cried Porbus, striking Poussin on the shoulder. "The flower of love soon fades, but the flower of art is immortal."

"Then am I only a woman now for him?" said Gillette. She was watching Poussin and Porbus closely.

She raised her head proudly; she glanced at Frenhofer, and her eyes flashed; then as she saw how her lover had fallen again to gazing at the portrait which he had taken at first for a Giorgione—

"Ah!" she cried; "let us go up to the studio. He never gave me such a look."

The sound of her voice recalled Poussin from his dreams.

"Old man," he said, "do you see this blade? I will plunge it into your heart at the first cry from this young girl; I will set fire to your house, and no one shall leave it alive. Do you understand?"

Nicolas Poussin scowled; every word was a menace. Gillette took comfort from the young painter's bearing, and yet more from that gesture, and almost forgave him for sacrificing her to his art and his glorious future.

Porbus and Poussin stood at the door of the studio and looked at each other in silence. At first the painter of the Saint Mary of Egypt hazarded some exclamations: "Ah! she has taken off her clothes; he told her to come into the light—he is comparing the two!" but the sight of the deep distress in Poussin's face suddenly silenced him; and though old painters no longer feel these scruples, so petty in the presence of art, he admired them because they were so natural and gracious in the lover. The young man kept his hand on the hilt of his dagger, and his ear was almost glued to the door. The two men standing in the shadow might have been conspirators waiting for the hour when they might strike down a tyrant.

"Come in, come in," cried the old man. He was radiant with delight. "My work is perfect. I can show her now with pride. Never shall painter, brushes, colors, light, and canvas produce a rival for 'Catherine Lescault,' the beautiful courtezan!"

Porbus and Poussin, burning with eager curiosity, hurried into a vast studio. Everything was in disorder and covered with dust, but they saw a few pictures here and there upon the wall. They stopped first of all in admiration before the life-size figure of a woman partially draped.

"Oh! never mind that," said Frenhofer; "that is a rough daub that I made, a study, a pose, it is nothing. These are my failures," he went on, indicating the enchanting compositions upon the walls of the studio.

This scorn for such works of art struck Porbus and Poussin dumb with amazement. They looked round for the picture of which he had spoken, and could not discover it.

"Look here!" said the old man. His hair was disordered, his face aglow with a more than human exaltation, his eyes glittered, he breathed hard like a young lover frenzied by love.

"Aha!" he cried, "you did not expect to see such perfection! You are looking for a picture, and you see a woman before you. There is such depth in that canvas, the atmosphere is so true that you can not distinguish it from the air that surrounds us. Where is art? Art has vanished, it is invisible! It is the form of a living girl that you see before you. Have I not caught the very hues of life, the spirit of the living line that defines the figure? Is there not the effect produced there like that which all natural objects present in the atmosphere about them, or fishes in the water? Do you see how the figure stands out against the background? Does it not seem to you that you pass your hand along the back? But then for seven years I studied and watched how the daylight blends with the objects on which it falls. And the hair, the light pours over it like a flood, does it not?... Ah! she breathed, I am sure that she breathed! Her breast—ah, see! Who would not fall on his knees before her? Her pulses throb. She will rise to her feet. Wait!"

"Do you see anything?" Poussin asked of Porbus.

"No... do you?"

"I see nothing."

The two painters left the old man to his ecstasy, and tried to ascertain whether the light that fell full upon the canvas had in some way neutralized all the effect for them. They moved to the right and left of the picture; they came in front, bending down and standing upright by turns.

"Yes, yes, it is really canvas," said Frenhofer, who mistook the nature of this minute investigation.

"Look! the canvas is on a stretcher, here is the easel; indeed, here are my colors, my brushes," and he took up a brush and held it out to them, all unsuspicious of their thought.

"The old *lansquenet* is laughing at us," said Poussin, coming once more toward the supposed picture. "I can see nothing there but confused masses of color and a multitude of fantastical lines that go to make a dead wall of paint."

"We are mistaken, look!" said Porbus.

In a corner of the canvas, as they came nearer, they distinguished a bare foot emerging from the chaos of color, half-tints and vague shadows that made up a dim, formless fog. Its living delicate beauty held them spellbound. This fragment that had escaped an incomprehensible, slow, and gradual destruction seemed to them like the Parian marble torso of some Venus emerging from the ashes of a ruined town.

"There is a woman beneath," exclaimed Porbus, calling Poussin's attention to the coats of paint with which the old artist had overlaid and concealed his work in the quest of perfection.

Both artists turned involuntarily to Frenhofer. They began to have some understanding, vague though it was, of the ecstasy in which he lived.

"He believes it in all good faith," said Porbus.

"Yes, my friend," said the old man, rousing himself from his dreams, "it needs faith, faith in art, and you must live for long with your work to produce such a creation. What toil some of those shadows have cost me. Look! there is a faint shadow there upon the cheek beneath the eyes—if you saw that on a human face, it would seem to you that you could never render it with paint. Do you think that that effect has not cost unheard of toil?

"But not only so, dear Porbus. Look closely at my work, and you will understand more clearly what I was saying as to methods of modeling and outline. Look at the high lights on the bosom, and see how by touch on touch, thickly laid on, I have raised the surface so that it catches the light itself and blends it with the lustrous whiteness of the high lights, and how by an opposite process, by flattening the surface of the paint, and leaving no trace of the passage of the brush, I have succeeded in softening the contours of my figures and enveloping them in half-tints until the very idea of drawing, of the means by which the effect is produced, fades away, and the picture has the roundness and relief of nature. Come closer. You will see the manner of working better; at a little distance it can not be seen. There I Just there, it is, I think, very plainly to be seen," and with the tip of his brush he pointed out a patch of transparent color to the two painters.

Porbus, laying a hand on the old artist's shoulder, turned to Poussin with a "Do you know that in him we see a very great painter?"

"He is even more of a poet than a painter," Poussin answered gravely.

"There," Porbus continued, as he touched the canvas, "Use the utmost limit of our art on earth."

"Beyond that point it loses itself in the skies," said Poussin.

"What joys lie there on this piece of canvas!" exclaimed Porbus.

The old man, deep in his own musings, smiled at the woman he alone beheld, and did not hear.

"But sooner or later he will find out that there is nothing there!" cried Poussin.

"Nothing on my canvas!" said Frenhofer, looking in turn at either painter and at his picture.

"What have you done?" muttered Porbus, turning to Poussin.

The old man clutched the young painter's arm and said, "Do you see nothing? clodpatel Huguenot! varlet! cullion! What brought you here into my studio? — My good Porbus," he went on, as he turned to the painter, "are you also making a fool of me? Answer! I am your friend. Tell me, have I ruined my picture after all?"

Porbus hesitated and said nothing, but there was such intolerable anxiety in the old man's white face that he pointed to the easel.

"Look!" he said.

Frenhofer looked for a moment at his picture, and staggered back.

"Nothing! nothing! After ten years of work..." He sat down and wept.

"So I am a dotard, a madman, I have neither talent nor power! I am only a rich man, who works for his own pleasure, and makes no progress, I have done nothing after all!"

He looked through his tears at his picture. Suddenly he rose and stood proudly before the two painters.

"By the body and blood of Christ," he cried with flashing eyes, "you are jealous! You would have me think that my picture is a failure because you want to steal her from me! Ah! I see her, I see her," he cried "she is marvelously beautiful..."

At that moment Poussin heard the sound of weeping; Gillette was crouching forgotten in a corner. All at once the painter once more became the lover. "What is it, my angel?" he asked her.

"Kill me!" she sobbed. "I must be a vile thing if I love you still, for I despise you.... I admire you, and I hate you! I love you, and I feel that I hate you even now!"

While Gillette's words sounded in Poussin's ears, Frenhof er drew a green serge covering over his "Catherine" with the sober deliberation of a jeweler who locks his drawers when he suspects his visitors to be expert thieves. He gave the two painters a profoundly astute glance that expressed to the full his suspicions, and his contempt for them, saw them out of his studio with impetuous haste and in silence, until from the threshold of his house he bade them "Good-by, my young friends!"

That farewell struck a chill of dread into the two painters. Porbus, in anxiety, went again on the morrow to see Frenhofer, and learned that he had died in the night after burning his canvases.

Paris, February, 1832.

9 781835 915516